FROM AN IDEA TO

NIKE

FROM AN IDEA TO

NIKE

How Marketing Made Nike a Global Success

LOWEY BUNDY SICHOL

illustrated by C. S. JENNINGS

HOUGHTON MIFFLIN HARCOURT
Boston   New York

hmhco.com

The text was set in ITC Galliard Std.

Library of Congress Cataloging-in-Publication Data
Names: Sichol, Lowey Bundy, author.
Title: From an idea to Nike : how marketing made Nike
a global success / by Lowey Bundy Sichol.
Description: Boston : Houghton Mifflin Harcourt, 2019. |
Series: From an idea to ... ; 2
Identifiers: LCCN 2018032035| ISBN 9781328453624 (hardcover) |
ISBN 9781328453631 (pbk.)
Subjects: LCSH: Nike (Firm)—History—Juvenile literature. |
Sporting goods industry—United States—History. | Footwear
industry—United States—History—Juvenile literature. | Athletic
shoes—United States—History—Juvenile literature. | Sports—
United States—Marketing—Juvenile literature.
Classification: LCC HD9992.U54 N5566 2019 | DDC 338.

Printed in the United States of America
DOC 10 9 8 7 6 5 4 3 2 1
4500745207

For Adam, my teammate in life.
Thank you for your love and support, and most
importantly, for always making me laugh.

Table of Contents

"Play by the rules. But be ferocious." —Phil Knight

Why does the Nike Swoosh appear virtually everywhere in the world of sports?

It may seem like every time you turn on a game, attend a sporting event, or read a sports story, all the athletes are wearing something or using equipment that displays the famous Nike Swoosh. It appears on shoes, uniforms, headbands, and equipment. For Nike, that's the winning strategy. Nike wants to be everywhere that athletes play and shop. But before Nike became a symbol for athletic success, it was just an idea by a man named Phil Knight.

Phil Knight was sitting in class one day at business school when his professor asked the students to come up with an idea for a new company. As you might guess, Phil's idea was a running shoe company. He had been a track star in high school and college, and he wanted to develop a superior running shoe at an affordable price.

Fast-forward several decades and Nike is not just an idea, it's the number one athletic shoe company in the world, with one of business's most successful marketing stories. This book tells the story of Nike— of how it grew from an idea into the world's most iconic sports company.

1 Phil Knight

Philip Hampson Knight was born in Portland, Oregon, on February 24, 1938. His parents, William and Lota, both grew up in terrible poverty but in other ways were quite different from each other. Lota was a beautiful woman yet extremely shy, and often kept her thoughts to herself. William,

"Everything you need is already inside." —Coach Bill Bowerman

on the other hand, was a small man with thick glasses, and was outspoken and tough. Through hard work, William became the publisher of a local newspaper called the *Oregon Journal*. William liked being admired by others, and often worried what people thought of him and his family.

The Knight family—Phil, his parents, and his twin sisters Joanne and Jeanne—lived in a big white house in a quiet suburb of Portland called Eastmoreland. Like his mother, Phil was very shy, an introvert. Absent-minded and often lost in his thoughts, Phil found comfort in one thing—sports. Phil's father also loved sports. In fact, it seemed that a passion for sports was the one thing Phil shared with his father. But William was relentless in his expectations, even when it came to his son's athletic activities. Phil felt that he was never able to please his father. Sometimes when Phil lost to his father in Ping-Pong, William laughed at him. This upset Phil so much that he would run out of the room in tears.

Over time, Phil became very competitive, perhaps because of his undying desire to make his father proud. Even at an early age, Phil did not like to lose. Once, when he and his cousin decided to play badminton in the backyard, Phil lost. Then he lost

again. And again. Phil lost 115 times in a row and didn't give up. Ultimately, he beat his cousin in the 116th game.

As a young child, Phil believed he'd grow up to become a professional baseball player—an accomplishment that would make his father very proud. But one day, Phil was cut from his high school baseball team. He was devastated, and sulked around the house for days. Finally, Phil's mother insisted he pull himself together and try out for a new sport.

"Like what?" Phil asked helplessly.

"How about track? You can run fast," his mother replied. Lota Knight was right. Phil could run fast. He tried out for the track team at Cleveland High School and not long after, the tall, thin blond was the number two runner in the state of Oregon.

Following high school, Phil attended the University of Oregon. He worked as a sports reporter for the *Oregon Daily Emerald* news-paper and ran for the University of Oregon track team.

Phil's coach was a legend, the most famous track coach in America—Bill Bowerman. Usually dressed in a tweed blazer, sweater vest, and string tie, he was extremely tough on his runners but also very dedicated to them. People both feared him and loved him. Phil admired Coach Bowerman and once said, "Besides my father there was no man whose

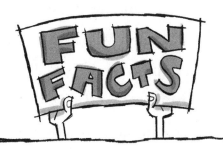

There are 5,280 feet in a mile. It takes a six-foot-tall runner approximately 880 steps to run one mile. According to Coach Bowerman, if he shaved one ounce off each running shoe, that would remove fifty-five pounds of weight over the course of a mile.

approval I craved more, and besides my father there was no man who gave it less often."

Coach Bowerman was also known for inventing lighter and more shock-absorbent running shoes for his team. Obsessed with shaving ounces from each shoe, he would tear apart several running shoes and reattach certain sections to create a better, slicker version.

ON THE STARTING LINE

In 1959, Phil Knight graduated from the University of Oregon. Although he had earned a bachelor's degree in journalism, he wasn't quite sure what he wanted to do with his life. In hopes of sorting things out, he enlisted in the army and served for one year.

At the end of that year, Phil decided to get a master's degree in business. He was accepted into the Stanford Graduate School of Business, one of the top-rated programs in the world.

Business school offers a high-level educational program for students who want to acquire skills like  leadership and teamwork and study business-specific subjects such as marketing, accounting, and finance. For the first time in his life, Phil was excited about something other than sports.

During his second year at Stanford, Phil took a class called **"Entrepreneurship,"** which taught students all about starting a new company. His professor, Frank Shallenberger, gave

Entrepreneurship: The act of starting a new business.

Entrepreneurs: People who take the risk of starting their own company in hopes of success.

the class an assignment: "Invent a new business, describe its purpose, and create a marketing plan."

A former track star himself, Phil naturally thought about running shoes. He did not believe that companies in the United States made good running shoes. At the time, two German companies, Adidas and Puma, dominated the

Industry: A group of companies that are related by what they sell or what service they provide.

athletic shoe **industry**, yet neither was focused on serious athletes like competitive runners with specialized needs.

Phil Knight's personal best time for one mile (1.6 km) was 4 minutes, 10 seconds. That's very fast!

Phil worked on his idea. He spent weeks researching and writing his entrepreneurship paper about a company that sold a superior running shoe. To help keep the shoes afford-able, they would be **manufactured** overseas in Asia, where labor was cheaper than in the United States or in Europe.

> **Manufactured:**
> Made or produced.

When the paper was written, Phil excitedly shared his idea with the rest of the class, yet they only "reacted with formal boredom." No one seemed to share Phil's enthusiasm, but for Phil, it didn't matter. He once said, "That class was an 'aha!' moment. First [Professor Frank] Shallenberger defined the type of person who was an entrepreneur—and I realized he was talking to me. I remember after writing that paper, saying to myself: 'This is really what I would like to do.'"

Phil wanted to start a company. More specifically, he wanted to start a running shoe company.

2 On Your Mark, Get Set . . .

After receiving a master of business administration (MBA) in 1962 from the Stanford Graduate School of Business, Phil Knight moved back home to live with his family. Time passed, and Phil's idea continued to brew in his mind. William Knight told him to forget about the running shoe idea and get a

"Dream audaciously. Have the courage to fail forward."
—Phil Knight

respectable job, perhaps as an accountant. Phil said he would, but first he wanted to travel, to see the world.

Reluctantly, William allowed his son to leave, and loaned him a little money. With it, Phil bought a plane ticket to Hawaii and then to Japan. While in Japan, Phil came across a high-quality low-cost running shoe called Tiger. Phil was so impressed with its quality that he contacted the manufacturer, a company called Onitsuka, which was located in Kobe.

A man named Ken Miyazaki, who worked for Mr. Onitsuka, agreed to a meeting.

Phil arrived at the meeting late (he had gone to the wrong place) and found Mr. Miyazaki, along with a dozen other Japanese businessmen, patiently waiting for him. Phil was nervous and scared, and had little money to make a deal. But he was also determined. Phil wanted the opportunity to buy Tiger running shoes and resell them in the United States through his own company. Mr. Miyazaki was intrigued with the idea, and asked Phil what company he worked for. Recalling his room filled with blue ribbons from track races, Phil

Onitsuka is now known as ASICS.

made up a name on the spot and replied, "Blue Ribbon Sports."

By the end of the meeting, Onitsuka and Phil had an agreement. Blue Ribbon Sports would sell Tiger shoes in the United States. Phil gave Onitsuka $50, and the company agreed to ship a small box of shoes to him in Oregon.

Since it would be some time before the shoes arrived in Oregon, Phil continued with

his trip around the world, visiting China, the Philippines, Thailand, Vietnam, Nepal, India, Kenya, Egypt, Turkey, Italy, France, and Germany.

On February 24, 1963, Phil returned home to Oregon. He was disappointed to learn that the shoes from Onitsuka still had not arrived. To pass the time and earn some money, Phil got a job as an accountant at a company called Lybrand, Ross Bros. & Montgomery. But he hated everything about the job and longed to work on his Blue Ribbon Sports idea. Finally, in early 1964, the shipment from Onitsuka arrived. The shoes were perfect!

Phil showed one of the pairs to Coach Bowerman and asked him what he thought. Coach Bowerman was impressed—so much so that he asked to be Phil's partner at Blue Ribbon Sports. Phil agreed, and, while most deals are sealed with legal documents, this one

was initially sealed with nothing more than a firm handshake.

On January 25, 1964, Phil Knight and Coach Bowerman officially started Blue Ribbon Sports. They each **invested** $500, and together they purchased three hundred pairs of Tiger

Invest: To give money to a company or project in hopes of making much more money in the future.

shoes, which they stored in the Blue Ribbon Sports warehouse, also known as the Knight family's basement.

WHAT IS MARKETING?

Marketing is the entire process from creating a product to selling it to the end consumer. Here are the four P's of marketing:

PRODUCT—What is your product? What does it do? Compared to similar products, how is it better, different, or newer? Don't forget about what's on the outside—your packaging creates the first impression you make on your customers and says a lot about what's inside. For example, yogurt companies created new sales opportunities when they added yogurt in new easy-to-carry squeezable packaging, like Go-Gurt® EZ Open Tubes.

PROMOTION—What promotions and advertising are running to help sell your product? What media are you using? Some possibilities include television, social media, radio, newspapers, direct mail, flyers, billboards, endorsements, public relations campaigns, and word of mouth.

PRICE—What is the price of your product, and what factors contribute to the price? How does your price compare with the price of similar products on the market? Is your product inexpensive, one that most people can afford (think Coca-Cola), a luxury product (think Rolls-Royce), or somewhere between these two?

PLACE—Where will you sell your product? In the grocery store, at a retail store, in a printed catalogue, online, or someplace else? Make sure it's easy for your customers to find and buy your product.

THE FIRST STEPS

Since Blue Ribbon Sports had no money to advertise, Phil started a **grassroots marketing**

> **Grassroots marketing:** Reaching out to a small, passionate group of prospective buyers in hopes that word will spread to a much larger group.

campaign. That meant he had to find dedicated runners and show them his running shoes in person. Fortunately, during the 1960s, Oregon was filled with passionate runners. Each weekend, Phil went to as many track meets as he possibly could. He talked to runners, listened to their feedback, and sold Tiger shoes from the trunk of his green Plymouth Valiant.

Runners went wild for Tiger shoes. They were well made and slick, and were designed for runners. Word spread, and when Phil wasn't selling shoes at a track meet, runners sometimes appeared at the Knights' family home in Eastmoreland, asking for Phil and his shoes. This embarrassed William, and he encouraged Phil to stop. But Phil was more determined than ever to prove himself right.

In the first year (1964), Blue Ribbon Sports sold about thirteen hundred pairs of Tiger running shoes, totaling $8,000 in **sales** but only $250 in **profits** (see page 29). The next year, Blue Ribbon Sports hired its first full-time employee, a fellow runner and hard-working salesman named Jeff Johnson. In 1965, sales hit $20,000 and profits jumped to $3,240. Meanwhile, Phil moved out of his parents' house and took a new job as an accountant at Price Waterhouse to help cover the costs incurred by operating Blue Ribbon Sports, the main expense being the purchase of shoes from Onitsuka.

In year three (1966), Blue Ribbon Sports opened its first store in Santa Monica, California. It sold a small selection of Tiger shoes and also acted as a gathering spot for serious runners in the area.

In year four (1967), Coach Bowerman designed a new running shoe that Onitsuka manufactured. It was called the Cortez. A superior distance training shoe, the Cortez was constructed with luxurious interior cushioning and a durable outer sole that could handle long runs. Thanks to a second store in Wellesley,  Massachusetts, and the excitement surrounding the Cortez, sales at Blue Ribbon Sports soared to $84,000.

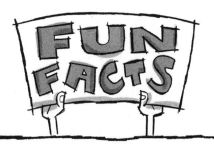

The earliest known shoes are sandals from approximately 8,000 B.C. They were found in Fort Rock Cave in Oregon, about two hundred miles from Phil Knight's Eastmoreland family home.

RUNNING TO THE ALTAR

Phil decided he could no longer handle simultaneously running Blue Ribbon Sports and managing the stressful demands of his job as an accountant, so he applied for and was offered a postion teaching accounting at a nearby college, Portland State University. Again, William Knight did not approve of his son's decisions, claiming that teaching was not a respectable profession. Phil took the job anyway and soon met a woman named Penny Parks. Penny was taking classes in accounting with the goal of building a better, more secure life for herself. She came from a large family with four siblings, a dog, cat, several monkeys, rats, and even a pet goose.

Like Phil, Penny was incredibly shy as well as determined and hard-working. Before long, Phil hired Penny as a part-time employee at Blue Ribbon Sports, where she helped with the invoicing, scheduling, and bookkeeping. Their friendship grew, and within a year, Phil and Penny were married.

PICKING UP THE PACE

While Phil was teaching accounting, spending time with Penny, and running Blue Ribbon Sports, Coach Bowerman continued to design trailblazing shoes. One

sneaker called the Boston launched in 1968 (year five) and featured a full-length midsole cushion. Coach Bowerman's **innovations** were changing the world of running!

Innovation: A revolutionary way of doing something. This could be a groundbreaking idea, a new method, or a pioneering product.

By the end of 1968, sales at Blue Ribbon Sports had hit $150,000. Phil Knight finally decided to quit his job teaching accounting and focus 100 percent on his running shoe company.

BUSINESS BASICS

What's the difference between sales and profits?

 **SALES**—Also called revenue. Sales consist of all the money that is collected from selling a product or service.

COSTS—Also called expenses or expenditures. Costs are the funds required to run a business or company. These include any direct costs incurred in the production of the goods sold, such as the price of materials used to make the product, the cost of labor and other salaries, and expenditures for rent and advertising.

 BREAKEVEN—The point reached when sales minus costs equals zero; in other words, the point at which total sales are equal to total costs.

PROFIT—The point at which sales minus costs equals a figure greater than zero.

Take, for example, a lemonade stand. Before you start selling lemonade, you'll need to buy cups ($3) and lemonade mix ($2). You borrow your mom's pitcher ($0). Your **costs** are $5. The price you decide to charge for each cup of lemonade is 50 cents.

If you sell ten cups of lemonade (ten x 50 cents), your **sales** will be $5. But that amount equals your **costs** (cups + lemonade mix = $5). At ten cups of lemonade, you **break even**. At eleven cups of lemonade sold, or $5.50, you now have made a **profit** of 50 cents. Keep selling to make more profit!

3 Go!

Word of Blue Ribbon Sports' groundbreaking running shoes traveled fast. The Cortez was a bestseller, and the company could barely keep up with demand. Blue Ribbon Sports was making a name for itself among runners and athletes. By 1971, the company had reached $1 million in sales and had a

"Few things are as crazy as my favorite thing, running. It's hard. It's painful. It's risky." —Phil Knight

few dozen employees. But its relationship with Onitsuka was in trouble.

A new **executive** at Onitsuka, named Shoji Katami, had taken over the relationship with Blue Ribbon Sports. Katami threatened Phil Knight. He said if Phil didn't sell Onitsuka 51 percent

Executive: An individual who holds a high position within a company and helps make major decisions.

of Blue Ribbon Sports, Onitsuka would find another U.S. company to buy and resell Tiger shoes in the United States.

Phil was furious. He also felt hurt. He

Nike, Precision Castparts, and Lithia Motors are the only Fortune 500 companies with headquarters in the state of Oregon.

had spent seven years selling Tiger shoes all over the United States. Not only that, Coach Bowerman had designed the company's most popular running shoes, the Cortez and the Boston. Phil did not want another U.S. company to sell these shoes *and* he did not want to sell any percentage of Blue Ribbon Sports to Onitsuka.

NIKE IS BORN

Phil went for a long run to clear his head. It was then that he had an idea. It was time to end the partnership with Onitsuka. Instead, Blue Ribbon Sports would run its own manufacturing plants and make all the shoes itself. But with the added responsibility of manufacturing, Phil decided that the company needed a new name.

Phil gathered his employees and shared his

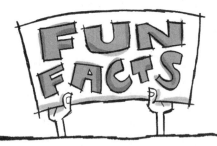

The name Nike was mispronounced early on—people thought it rhymed with Mike. So Nike changed the typeface on its products from all lowercase letters (nike) to all capital letters (NIKE).

vision. "This is the moment we've been waiting for," he said. "Our moment. No more selling someone else's brand." It was time to create a new brand that would be all their own.

First, the company needed a new **logo**.

Logo: A picture or symbol that a company uses to represent itself. Logos come in all shapes, sizes, and colors. Some famous logos include the McDonald's golden arches and the cursive, red Coca-Cola name.

Phil wanted it to evoke a sense of running . . . a sense of motion . . . a sense of victory. He wanted it to be different, exciting, and time-less. And it had to fit on the side of a running shoe.

Phil hired Carolyn Davidson, a graphic design student at Portland State University, to create the logo. When Carolyn returned with

sketches, one design popped out to several of the employees—what appeared to be a curved, fat check mark. While Phil didn't really like it, he thanked Carolyn for her work and paid her $35.

Now that the logo was chosen, the company needed a new name. Again, Phil gathered his employees and asked for ideas. Phil strongly suggested the name Dimension Six. His employees did not like this name and voted for

Falcon instead. Phil was running out of time. Neither name felt right, and the new shoes were about to be shipped from the factory. They needed a name fast. Then Jeff Johnson, the first full-time employee Phil had hired, suggested that the company be named Nike, for the Greek goddess of victory. Jeff explained that the name had come to him in a dream the night before. At the time, Phil announced, "Well, I don't really like it that much . . . Hopefully, it will grow on us."

Carolyn Davidson, the Portland State University student who designed the Nike Swoosh, was once asked to name the second biggest project she ever worked on. She replied, "Wallpaper for a Walla Walla motel."

Next came packaging . . . Phil wanted it to be bold, and to stand out from the packaging used by Adidas and Puma. Until then, all shoe boxes had been blue or white, so Phil asked that the Nike shoes be placed in bright orange boxes with a white "nike" in lowercase letters, and the Swoosh on the side.

On May 30, 1971, Nike and its new logo officially launched to the world.

4 Off to the Races

In the 1970s, very few runners had athletic endorsement deals, and Nike used that to its advantage. An endorsement deal is an agreement between a company and a well-liked and well-known individual, often an athlete, actor, or musician. Its purpose is to use an individual's popularity and fame to persuade

"Success isn't how far you got, but the distance you traveled from where you started." —Steve "Pre" Prefontaine

others to buy a company's product or brand. In return, the company pays the celebrity or athlete money.

Phil believed that other runners would want to wear the shoes worn by the best runners in the world. In 1972, members of Nike's team showed up at the Olympic track-and-field trials at Hayward Field in Eugene, Oregon, and gave away Nike shoes and T-shirts to any athlete who would take them. Several athletes competed and did well in Nike shoes, but Phil

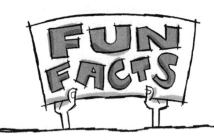

Steve Prefontaine broke the American record for the 5,000-meter race on July 6, 1972, with a time of 13 minutes, 22.8 seconds. His record stood for 40 years, until Galen Rupp broke it in 2012 with a speed of 13 minutes, 22.67 seconds.

had his eyes set on one runner in particular—Steve Prefontaine. Known to all as "Pre," he was the fastest runner alive. He had run at the University of Oregon, and Coach Bowerman had called him "the best runner I've ever had." With his bushy mop of hair, thick, dark mustache, and strong, lean legs, Pre was an icon in the world of running.

While at the University of Oregon, Pre dominated every race he ran, ultimately winning seven National Collegiate Athletic Association (NCAA) titles—three in cross-country and four in track. He then went on to break every American record for races between two miles and six miles and between two thousand and ten thousand meters. And he did it with arrogant confidence. Pre was outspoken and competitive, and didn't care what others thought of him. He was Nike's perfect athletic endorser.

In 1973, Nike paid Pre $5,000 yearly to endorse Nike products. Just like his running style, Pre endorsed Nike with hard work, determination, and a competitive drive. He wore Nike T-shirts wherever he went, spoke passionately about the company, and sent Nike shoes to fellow runners, with lots of encouragement to wear them. By the end of 1973, Nike's sales hit $4.8 million.

On May 30, 1975, Phil got a call in the early morning hours. Pre had tragically died in a car accident. He was twenty-four years old. Phil and the rest of the running world were devastated.

RUNNING WITH OTHERS

Nike went on to sign athletic endorsement deals with many other elite runners throughout the 1970s, including six-foot-two Jon

Nike made its first athletic endorsement deal in 1972, and not with a runner. Nike signed an Olympic welterweight wrestler named Wayne Wells, who wore a custom-made high-top Nike wrestling boot.

Anderson, who won the Boston Marathon in a pair of Nikes, and Alberto Salazar, who laced up his Nike shoes to triumph in three New York City marathons. Runners preferred to sign with Nike instead of other shoe companies for several reasons. For one thing, Nike spent a lot of time at track meets and had strong relationships with many of the world's top runners. Every time Nike talked to runners, it was conducting **market research** by listening

Market research: Information gathered about consumers' needs and preferences. This knowledge can be gathered formally, through a questionnaire or focus group, or informally, as Nike did when it spoke with runners at track meets.

to **consumers'** feedback, concerns, and needs. In addition, most of Nike's employees were passionate runners themselves, so elite runners believed that Nike understood them. Perhaps most important, Nike's innovative running shoes were unlike any other shoe on the market. They were the best.

The first athletic endorsement deals occurred in the early 1900s, mostly with golfers and baseball players. Babe Ruth, the legendary player for the Red Sox and Yankees, had agreements with several tobacco and candy companies. Another "Babe"—Babe Didrikson Zaharias—was an All-American female basketball player, two-time Olympic gold medalist in track and field, and cofounder and ten-time champion of the Ladies Professional Golf Association. In the 1940s, she was sponsored by Chrysler automobiles and Wheaties.

5 Waffle Iron Inspiration

Coach Bowerman continued to invent new shoes for Nike. The inspiration for his most famous shoe came to him one morning during a breakfast of waffles. A brand-new track had just been installed at the University of Oregon, and Coach Bowerman wanted to design a shoe that would grip the track's surface

"The way to stay ahead was through product innovation. We happen to be great at it." —Phil Knight

better than other shoes. Gazing at his wife's waffle iron that morning, the coach envisioned the bottom of a shoe looking just like it. He believed a "waffle iron sole" would grip any ground better, whether it was a rubber track, dirt, or grass, and would produce superior running results. Excited about his new idea, Coach Bowerman decided to test it. He ran into his garage and grabbed two cans of chemicals to create melted urethane—a kind of rubber he

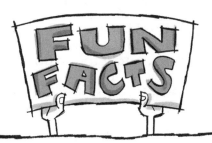

Nike Headquarters in Beaverton, Oregon, are located at One Bowerman Drive, named after cofounder Coach Bill Bowerman. There, many Nike artifacts from more than half a century of business are on display, including Coach Bowerman's ruined waffle iron.

used to make soles—then poured the contents of the cans into his wife's waffle iron. The initial results were not good. He had forgotten to add an anti-stick agent and had glued the waffle iron shut, completely ruining it. Coach Bowerman ran out and bought another waffle

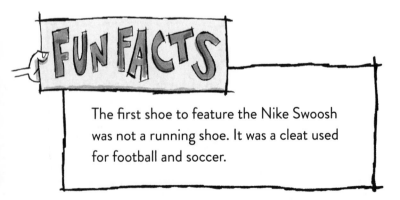

FUN FACTS

The first shoe to feature the Nike Swoosh was not a running shoe. It was a cleat used for football and soccer.

iron, but this time he poured plaster into it. Again the mold wasn't perfect and melted, but he didn't give up.

Fortunately, Nike's engineers had better luck. They created a durable waffle mold that led to Nike's newest shoe. In 1974, Nike launched the Waffle Trainer, which featured a **patented**, unique bottom sole and soon became the nation's best-selling shoe. Between the success of the Waffle Trainer and the company's athletic endorsements, sales continued to rise.

Patent: A form of protection, issued by the government, so others can't steal someone's idea for a new product, invention, or innovative way of doing something.

6 Stumbling

In 1980, Nike had about twenty-seven hundred employees and $270 million in sales, and it had hit a milestone. It had passed Adidas in sales and was the number one athletic shoe company in the United States. In that same year, Nike **went public** (see pages 54–55). Individuals could now invest their

"You've got to worry about what's coming up to stay ahead of the curve." —Phil Knight

money in Nike by buying shares of the company's stock.

Despite the exciting milestone, something was changing. Executives at Nike sensed a shift in fashion trends and tastes in athletic shoes. People, in general, didn't care as much about Nike's focus on innovation or the endorsements that came mostly from young male runners. In addition, fewer people were showing an interest in running. Instead, fitness and aerobics were quickly growing in popularity.

Women led the new trend in fitness, and a company called Reebok surged onto the

FUN FACTS

Nike went public on December 2, 1980. Another iconic company, Apple, went public the following week, on December 12.

market with a new batch of fashionable aerobic shoes made from soft leather. Phil explained, "Reebok came out of nowhere to dominate the aerobics market, which we completely miscalculated . . . Reebok's shoe was sleek and attractive, while ours was sturdy and clunky. By the time we developed a leather that was both strong and soft, Reebok had established a brand, won a huge chunk of sales, and gained the momentum to go right by us."

Nike was in trouble.

In 1984, just four years after going public, Nike had its first set of **layoffs** and, for the first time ever, the company was not profitable. Sales plummeted. In 1986, just two years later, Reebok passed Nike to become the number one athletic shoe company in the United States. Something had to change . . .

FUN FACTS

In some cultures, it's considered good luck to throw a shoe at a person as he or she leaves for a journey, but in Arab cultures, it's an insult to show another person the sole of one's shoe.

WHAT DOES "GOING PUBLIC" MEAN?

Every new company starts off as a **private company** or a **privately held company**. That means the founders who started their business own the entire company and run it the way they want. The founders make all the key decisions for the company. These decisions are private information and not shared with the public.

Some founders may want to switch from being a private company to being a **public company** or a **publicly held company**. When a company goes public, it can raise a lot of money by selling off "**shares of stock**," or bits of ownership, to anyone wh is willing to pay the price. That means the *public* will now own part of the company.

One way to think about going public is to think of a company as a building. Each brick of the building is like a share of stock.

1.50 MILLION BRICKS →

When a company is private, the founders and private investors own all the bricks of the building (or the entire company).

When a company goes public, the founders and private investors sell off a specific number of bricks (or shares of stock) for money—so other people now have a chance to own some of the company. The people who buy and own these shares are called **shareholders**. The price for each brick (or share) can range from a few cents to thousands of dollars based on how well the company is doing. The more each brick (or share) is worth, the more valuable the building (or company) is worth.

WHY DO STOCK PRICES GO UP AND DOWN?

A company can have a high or low stock price for many reasons. A high stock price usually means the company's products are selling well, it is making lots of money, and good leaders are in place. Most people want to own shares of stock in a company that is doing very well and is expected to grow bigger, so the price goes up.

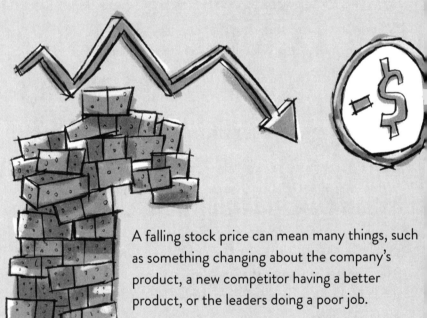

A falling stock price can mean many things, such as something changing about the company's product, a new competitor having a better product, or the leaders doing a poor job.

The more shares someone holds in one company, the more ownership he or she possesses. For example, when Phil retired in 2016, he was Nike's largest shareholder, owning 24.2 million shares worth $32.1 billion!

WHY DO COMPANIES GO PUBLIC?

The main reason companies decide to go public is to raise money. They can use this money to expand into new areas, develop new products, acquire new companies, hire more people, or pay off debt.

That might sound like a good deal, but there are challenges, too. When a company goes public, there are lots (sometimes tens of millions) of people who now own a little bit of the company. In addition, a public company must follow the rules and regulations set by a department of the U.S. government called the Securities and Exchange Commission (SEC).

The job of the SEC is to protect investors from any sort of dishonest business. The SEC makes and enforces strict rules and regulations that all public companies must follow.

Not every company believes going public is worth the effort of having to follow these rules and regulations or sharing its company information with the public.

7 Michael Jordan: Another Perfect Fit

Before the 1980s, Nike had never run a major advertising campaign. The company relied on athletic endorsements from runners and small ads in running magazines. But when aerobics, fitness, and style combined to create a new trend, many people—women in particular—no longer felt a connection to

"You can't explain much in 60 seconds, but when you show Michael Jordan, you don't have to. It's that simple." —Phil Knight

Nike. Sales were falling fast, and Nike needed to turn things around. It needed to become more current and in touch with consumers. It needed to do some advertising.

Phil met with a small advertising agency near Beaverton, Oregon, called Wieden+Kennedy. Phil introduced himself by saying, "Hi. I'm Phil Knight, and I don't believe in advertising." Dan Wieden, the president of the

Nike's first commercial for the Air Max shoe ran in 1987 and used the original recording of the Beatles' song "Revolution" as its soundtrack. Nike had paid EMI-Capitol Records (which had previously purchased the song) $250,000 to use "Revolution" in its ads. The Beatles were furious that their classic song was being used to sell a product, and sued Nike for $15 million.

firm, smiled, knowing he would soon change Phil's mind.

Wieden+Kennedy believed Nike could gain back consumers and grow if it expanded into a sport that was hot and growing in popularity. So it turned Nike's focus to basketball. In particular, the agency recommended that Nike sponsor a basketball player, someone who was on the verge of becoming the sport's next big star . . .

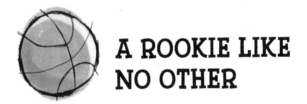

A ROOKIE LIKE NO OTHER

In 1984, Michael Jordan was a basketball standout from the University of North Carolina. He had dominated in the NCAA, helping the University of Carolina win the

national title, and in the 1984 Olympics, leading the team to a gold medal victory. On June 19, 1984, Michael Jordan turned pro when the Chicago Bulls selected him during the National Basketball Association (NBA) draft.

As a pro, the twenty-one-year-old was eager

to sign an endorsement deal with Adidas, his favorite basketball shoe company. But Adidas was in a period of transition. The company's founder, Adi Dassler, had passed away in 1978, and his wife, Käthe, who had become president of Adidas at the time of her husband's passing, had fallen ill. Käthe died at the end of 1984. Needless to say, Adidas was not focused on doing a deal with Michael Jordan. But Nike was.

Back home, Michael Jordan insisted that he wanted a deal with Adidas, not Nike. However, he grudgingly agreed to fly to Beaverton, Oregon, to meet with Nike's executives.

While at Nike Headquarters, Jordan learned all about the company. Nike's focus on innovation impressed him. Jordan had never worn Nike shoes, but the company promised to custom fit a shoe just for him, something that had never before been done for a basketball player.

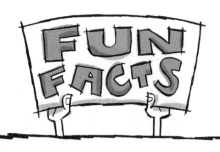

Michael Jordan no longer plays professional basketball, but his shoes are still very much in demand. As a result, he earns $110 million from Nike each year and another $40 million annually from other companies, such as Gatorade, Coca-Cola, and McDonald's. Even though he has retired from professional basketball, Michael Jordan is still the highest paid athlete in the world!

Nike offered to pay Michael Jordan $500,000 every year for five years. Prior to this, the most any company had paid a basketball player was $150,000 per year. Nike also promised to run a million-dollar advertising campaign supporting Michael Jordan's new Nike basketball shoe. As a final incentive, Nike offered Jordan a brand-new Mercedes.

Jordan couldn't resist. It was a deal!

AIR JORDANS ARE A SLAM DUNK

The first Nike basketball shoe made for Michael Jordan (it was not yet called the Air Jordan) launched on October 15, 1984. Just three days later, the NBA banned the shoe, stating its red-and-black colors were too bright and didn't properly match other uniform shoes, which were white and black. The NBA fined Jordan $5,000 for every game in which he wore his red-and-black Nike basketball shoes. Nike happily paid the fine for Jordan, because the media attention surrounding him was worth much more than $5,000 per game. Then Nike released a television commercial that announced *"On October 15, Nike created a revolutionary new basketball shoe. On October 18, the NBA*

threw them out of the game. Fortunately, the NBA can't keep you from wearing them."

Kids and teenagers couldn't wait to wear the same Nike shoe as the rebellious rookie sensation who could fly across the court and slam-dunk over everyone's head.

In 1985, Nike created the Air Jordan I with

its own unique logo, a silhouette of Michael Jordan flying across the air with a basketball palmed high in his left hand. That logo still exists today. The Air Jordan I came in black, red, and white and cost $65. It was the most expensive basketball shoe on the market.

One of the first television commercials for Air Jordan I was filmed in slow motion. It captured a basketball rolling along an outdoor court. As the sound of jet engines revved in the background, Jordan picked up the ball and drove toward the basket. The sound of engines increased in volume as Jordan sailed through the air and slam-dunked the ball over the camera. The slow-motion commercial electrified the Air Jordan campaign.

Thanks to Nike's

creative advertising and Jordan's sensational rookie season, Nike sold $100 million of Air Jordan shoes in their first year on the market. That year alone, Michael Jordan averaged 28.2 points per game and was named Rookie of the Year. Even better, Gatorade launched a campaign encouraging boys and girls to "Be Like Mike." Michael Jordan was on his way to becoming the greatest basketball player in the world. He would eventually win six NBA championships, five NBA Most Valuable Player awards, and many other honors, and would do it all in Nike shoes.

FUN FACTS

Sneakers were invented in the 1800s. They got their name because people could "sneak" around in them—the rubber soles didn't make a sound.

8 Just Do It

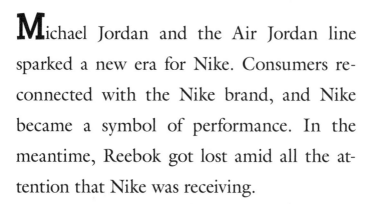

Michael Jordan and the Air Jordan line sparked a new era for Nike. Consumers reconnected with the Nike brand, and Nike became a symbol of performance. In the meantime, Reebok got lost amid all the attention that Nike was receiving.

In 1988, Nike introduced a new

"The final game of the NCAA Basketball Tournament is better than any runway in Paris for launching a shoe." —Phil Knight

$20 million marketing campaign called "Just Do It." The now famous **tagline** featured hard-working, determined athletes across many sports. The ads were powerful and emotional and spoke to everyone—from elite atheletes to children. Many Just Do It ads played up the company's rebellious and aggressive approach to marketing, sometimes employing harsh

Tagline: A group of words or a short slogan that helps communicate a company's message. Taglines appear throughout advertising campaigns.

The Just Do It campaign is now enshrined as part of America's story at the Smithsonian National Museum.

images. There were shots of a boxer losing his mouthpiece after a punch to the face and a runner throwing up all over his Nike shoes after winning a marathon. By 1990, Nike's sales had surpassed $2 billion in the United States, and Nike was back on top as the country's number one athletic shoe company.

Meanwhile, Nike signed many more athletes and teams to endorsement deals. The company wanted its logo to appear anywhere there might be a moment of athletic greatness. In 1993, Nike had deals with 265 NBA basketball players, 275 NFL football players, and 290 MLB baseball players. In addition, Nike sponsored many of the winning teams in NCAA college basketball.

9 Running Around the World

Nike dominated the U.S. athletic shoe market in the 1990s, but Phil had his eyes on a bigger prize—selling beyond U.S. borders. In particular, he wanted to expand into Europe, where Adidas was number one. Adidas was headquartered in Germany, and Phil knew it would be much harder to beat a competitor

"Perceptions can be changed."
—Phil Knight

on its own turf outside the United States.

NIKE KICKS OFF IN EUROPE

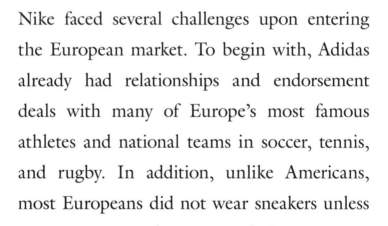

Nike faced several challenges upon entering the European market. To begin with, Adidas already had relationships and endorsement deals with many of Europe's most famous athletes and national teams in soccer, tennis, and rugby. In addition, unlike Americans, most Europeans did not wear sneakers unless they were playing a sport. Sneakers were worn only on the field, track, or tennis court. And finally, Europeans did not take to

Nike's Just Do It campaign. To them, it came off as aggressive and arrogant. Nike would need a new marketing strategy if it was to succeed in Europe.

As a first step toward connecting with European consumers, Nike created a different set of Just Do It commercials. The new ads showed inspirational images of everyday people, such as kids playing soccer in the streets or a runner jogging alongside a strip of peaceful, beautiful scenery.

Next, Nike signed deals with European track-and-field athletes in hopes of building connections with their fans. Nike also had to find a way to engage with soccer—Europe's most popular sport. Since Adidas already sponsored most of the national soccer teams, Nike decided to sponsor youth soccer leagues and smaller local teams.

In 1994, Nike had a stroke of good luck when Brazil won the World Cup. At that time,

Brazil was the only national team worldwide in which several players wore Nike soccer  cleats. The World Cup victory helped Nike gain credibility and respect among soccer fans all over the world. Soon after, Nike made deals with both the men's and women's national soccer teams in the United States and with the national teams in Italy, Nigeria, and Brazil. Nike had suddenly become a big player in the world of soccer.

FUN FACTS

Soccer is the world's most popular sport, with an estimated global following of more than 4 billion fans. The next most popular sport worldwide is cricket, with 2.5 billion fans, succeeded by field hockey, with 2 billion fans, and tennis, with 1 billion enthusiasts.

10 Tiger Woods Drives Nike Golf

In 1996, Nike moved fast to sign an endorsement deal with a rising golf star. At the time, the company didn't make or sell anything related to golf, but that didn't matter. Nike saw a unique opportunity in Tiger Woods—a phenomenal athlete who was on the verge of greatness.

"Make history or be a part of it."
—Phil Knight

As a toddler, Tiger Woods learned to play golf from his father, Earl, an African American retired lieutenant colonel and Vietnam War veteran. Tiger's mother, Kultida Punsawad, was from Thailand. Tiger once referred to his ethnic makeup as "Cablinasian"—a term he invented to represent the blending of his **Ca**ucasian, **Bl**ack, American **In**dian, and **Asian** genetic makeup. By the age of eight, Tiger was winning tournaments around the country. He won the Junior World Golf Championship six times before turning pro at the age of twenty.

Tiger and the Nike brand were an ideal fit. Tiger had the potential to shatter records and break down stereotypes in the traditionally conservative sport of golf. He brought excitement and new, more diverse players and fans to the game. He exemplified the spirit of Nike.

In 1996, Nike agreed to pay Tiger $40 million for a five-year contract. Then the company created a business division called Nike Golf. The new division launched with Tiger using a specially designed Nike Tour Accuracy ball and wearing Nike golf apparel. The Nike Swoosh appeared on Tiger's hat and shirt, and on the

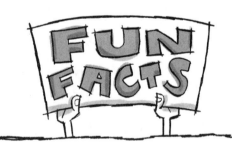

When Tiger was two years old, he appeared on TV's *The Mike Douglas Show,* and had a putting contest with the famous comedian Bob Hope. Tiger picked up his ball and moved it a few inches from the hole, then tapped it in.

golf balls he used. For many years, Tiger also played exclusively with Nike golf clubs—even after the company announced it would stop selling golf equipment in 2016. And he established a new tradition: on the last day of each tournament he played in, he wore a red Nike shirt emblazoned with the Nike Swoosh.

A MAJOR CHAMPION

In golf, there are four tournaments called "the majors"—the Masters, in April; the PGA

Championship, in May; the U.S. Open, in June; and The Open Championship (sometimes re-ferred to as the British Open), in July. When a golfer wins all four tournaments in four con-secutive victories, it's called a Grand Slam.

Tiger won his first major, the Masters, in 1997, with a record-breaking twelve-stroke lead. At the age of twenty-four, he became the youngest golfer ever to win each of the four majors—a career Grand Slam. In total, he has won fourteen major golf champion-ships—the highest achievement of any player after Jack Nicklaus. Over the course of his ca-reer Tiger has broken many records, including being ranked number one for 271 consecutive weeks and being ranked number one for a total of 683 weeks.

Tiger was also named PGA Tour Player of the Year eleven times—more than any other golfer.

Tiger's victories took the game of golf to a new level of excitement. Instead of being quiet and polite in the traditional manner, Tiger fans hooted and hollered after each shot, bringing energy and youthfulness to golf courses everywhere that Tiger played. Along the way, sales of Nike golf equipment and apparel took off. After each Tiger victory, for example, Nike golf balls sold out and the shirt and pants he wore at tournaments flew off the shelves.

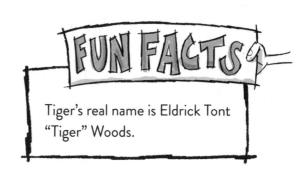

FUN FACTS

Tiger's real name is Eldrick Tont "Tiger" Woods.

Nike re-signed Tiger Woods with a $100 million five-year contract for the years 2001 to 2006. But no one expected the deal to accomplish what it did during the 2005 Masters in what's been called the "greatest moment of unplanned advertising ever." After studying a very difficult chip shot for several minutes, Tiger hit from the edge of the rough. His Nike ball rolled 25 feet before turning sharply down a steep break. With the cameras rolling, the ball slowly approached the hole and settled on the lip of the cup for almost a full two seconds—with the black Swoosh in plain view—before dropping into the hole for a birdie. The crowd went

wild. Tiger's sensational chip shot was replayed so many times over news and sports broadcasts that marketing experts estimated Nike received more than $1 million in free advertising from that one chip shot!

Tiger was even more popular in Asia than he was in the United States. He helped drive Nike sales all around the world. In 2003, the company hit another milestone. Nike had earned $5.1 billion in international sales (in Europe, Asia, and South America) and $4.6 billion in U.S. sales. For the first time, Nike's international sales had exceeded its domestic sales.

11 Cheaters Never Win

Signing popular athletes or other celebrities to endorsement deals is a great strategy for building brand or product awareness and credibility. But what happens if the celebrity makes bad decisions?

Lance Armstrong was born in 1971 and was an elite athlete at a young age. When

"Nike is not about going to a ball game. It's a business. People don't always realize that we take things seriously." —Phil Knight

he was thirteen years old, he competed in the IronKids Triathlon. At twenty-two, he won the World Championships Road Race. In 1996, Nike signed a deal with Armstrong in hopes of driving sales in Nike cycling. But later that same year, Armstrong became ill and was diagnosed with a very serious form of cancer, which had spread to his lungs, brain, and abdomen. At twenty-five years old, he was given little chance of survival.

But Lance Armstrong did survive. Not only that, he returned to cycling and won the

Tour de France, the world's most famous cycling race, seven years in a row, from 1999 to 2005. He also won the bronze medal in the 2000 Olympic Games in Sydney. For many years, Lance Armstrong was considered the greatest cyclist of all time.

During Lance Armstrong's reign as a cycling phenomenon, Nike sold millions of dollars of biking apparel and gear. In addition, Nike aligned with the Livestrong Foundation, the charity Armstrong established to help fight cancer. Nike sold about 80 million yellow LIVESTRONG bracelets and raised more

FUN FACTS

Lance Armstrong was also an accomplished swimmer. At the age of twelve, he placed fourth in the Texas State 1500-meter freestyle.

than $100 million for the charity. It seemed like yet another winning athletic endorsement deal for Nike.

Then, in 2012, everything changed. The U.S. Anti-Doping Agency investigation concluded that Lance Armstrong had used illegal performance-enhancing drugs over the course of his cycling career. The punishment? Armstrong was banned from cycling, triathlons, and other sports and stripped of every single title he had won, starting in 1998. That meant that he was stripped of his seven Tour de France titles. It was the biggest scandal in sports.

Nike no longer felt that Lance Armstrong's conduct was aligned with its company values. Armstrong had cheated, lied, and used illegal drugs. Nike ended Armstrong's endorsement deal, stating that "Nike does not condone the use of illegal performance-enhancing drugs in any manner."

Other Nike-endorsed athletes have struggled with personal problems without necessarily losing their endorsement deal with the company. For example, Tiger Woods struggled with family troubles in 2008 and was arrested for driving under the influence of painkillers in 2017. While both of these were serious offenses, Nike stood by Tiger Woods, since his behavior was personal, and not directly tied to his performance on the golf course.

12 Leader of the Pack

Staying number one in the world of athletic shoes for so many years has been a challenge. Nike faces tough competition from many companies. Adidas and Reebok have battled with Nike since the early days. Puma, Fila, and New Balance are also strong rivals. And

"Don't give anything away. Never make it easy for the guys you are trying to beat." —Coach Bill Bowerman

lately, Nike has felt the heat from a hot new company called Under Armour.

Under Armour was founded in 1996 by Kevin Plank, a former University of Maryland football player. As a fullback, he had grown tired of having to change out of the sweaty, heavy cotton shirts he wore under his jersey. He wanted to make athletic shirts that would use a moisture-wicking synthetic fabric. After his graduation from the University of Maryland,

Nike's world headquarters in Beaverton, Oregon, are surrounded by two hundred acres of woods and several ball fields. The campus buildings are named for some of Nike's most influential athletic endorsers—Steve Prefontaine, Mia Hamm, Ken Griffey Jr., Tiger Woods, Jerry Rice, and Michael Jordan, among others.

Kevin developed his first prototype of the revolutionary shirt that would keep athletes cool  and dry. Today, Under Armour sells athletic clothing, shoes, and gear. And, like Nike, it sponsors elite athletes and teams, including NBA Most Valuable Player Stephen Curry, New England Patriots superstar quarterback Tom Brady, golf sensation Jordan Spieth, and Olympic skier Lindsey Vonn.

A PERSONAL BEST

Staying ahead of companies like Adidas and Under Armour means Nike must continue to have the best marketing and most innovative

products. In recent years, Nike has focused on targeting consumers on a personal level through digital marketing. Nike's running app, Nike+ (Nike Plus), connects with millions of runners every day. With features like training tips and individualized goal setting, Nike+ records every activity so users can track their progress, share runs, challenge friends, and post accomplishments on social media. Nike even creates personalized recommendations for shoes and gear based on users' activities and profiles.

RUNNING DIFFERENT CHANNELS

Nike leverages its strong **distribution channels** to help stay ahead of the competition. That means there are several simple ways for consumers to buy Nike products.

> **Distribution channel:** A business that moves products or services to the next step on the chain, i.e. retail stores, wholesalers, catalogues, and the internet.

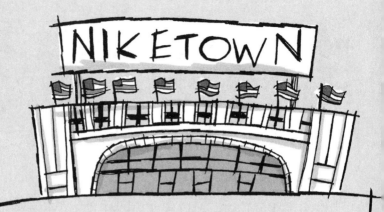

NIKETOWN: Nike launched its flagship stores, Niketown, in 1990. These all-Nike stores are located in prime metropolitan shopping areas, such as Michigan Avenue in Chicago and Newbury Street in Boston, and give Nike an opportunity to feature, display, and control its products the way it wants. The world's largest Niketown, on Oxford Street in London, England, spans 42,000 square feet on four floors and offers a custom soccer-shoe molding machine and embroidery service. Players can have their name, number, and even national flag stitched onto their shoes.

RETAIL: Nike sells its products through other retailers' stores. These are primarily sports, clothing, and shoe stores such as Foot Locker, Finish Line, and Dick's Sporting Goods.

ONLINE: Nike's online store, Nike.com, sells a wide range of Nike products. On NikeID.com, consumers can customize their own shoes and gear with a variety of styles, materials, and colors. Outside retailers, such as Zappos and Amazon, also sell Nike products through their websites.

CATALOGUES: Nike's products appear in shoe, sporting goods, and clothing catalogues.

NIKE FACTORY STORES: Nike Factory stores sell Nike products at a discounted price. There are more than two hundred Nike Factory stores in the United States and more than five hundred of these stores throughout the rest of the world.

SPECIALTY STORES: Nike operates specialized running stores and basketball stores. Nike's running stores provide additional services such as workshops and training sessions. Nike partnered with Foot Locker to create specialty basketball stores called the House of Hoops. There, fans and customers can watch highlight clips, customize T-shirts, and purchase limited-edition basketball footwear.

13 Running Nike Today

Nike started as an idea to sell high-quality running shoes *for* athletes *by* athletes. It launched in running, the area Phil knew best, and gained credibility by connecting with runners, first at track meets and later through endorsement deals with elite runners. Next, the company expanded across other sports,

"The most important thing we do is market the product." —Phil Knight

including basketball, soccer, golf, and cycling. The athletic endorsements that it signed created credibility and a wider following, while powerful marketing campaigns developed an emotional bond between the Nike brand and consumers. Along the way, Nike learned that one marketing message does not fit all. As the company expanded into new sports and new countries, it had to adapt its marketing to show that it understood the needs of different athletes, sports, and cultures.

Today, Nike is a marketing powerhouse. The company spends more than $3 billion

FUN FACTS

Nike's mission is "to bring inspiration and innovation to every athlete in the world."

each year on endorsements, brand events, and television, digital, and print advertising. The Nike Swoosh appears on everything from jerseys to wristwatches to skateboards to swim caps to backpacks. As a result, Nike has made itself a symbol of athletic performance. Kids still want to fly like Michael Jordan, slam-dunk like LeBron James, smash an overhead like Serena Williams, and score a goal like Neymar Jr. Maybe it's not surprising that consumers worldwide spend $50 million on Nike shoes each day.

Nike is now led by a new team of people. Coach Bill Bowerman died in 1999 at the age of eighty-eight. Phil Knight stepped down as CEO in 2004 and as chairman in 2016. But the spirit of these two founders lives tirelessly within the halls of Nike's headquarters and wherever Nike athletic shoes and apparel are sold.

Over the years, Phil and Penny Knight have donated hundreds of millions of dollars to Stanford University and the University of Oregon—the places that inspired Phil to create Nike. At the University of Oregon, a new athletic center is dedicated to Phil's and Penny's mothers, and a plaque next to the entrance reads BECAUSE MOTHERS ARE OUR FIRST COACHES. Ideas can come from anywhere. Who knows if Nike would have existed if Phil's mother hadn't suggested that he try out for track that one day.

TIMELINE OF NIKE

1938 • Philip H. Knight is born in Portland, Oregon, on February 24.

1954 • Phil is one of the top high school runners in Oregon.

1955 • Phil attends the University of Oregon. He runs for the varsity track team and the legendary coach Bill Bowerman.

1959 • Phil graduates from the University of Oregon.

1960 • Phil enrolls in the Stanford Graduate School of Business. While there, he takes a class on entrepreneurship and comes up with the idea to create a high-quality running shoe company that manufactures its shoes overseas.

1962 • Phil travels to Japan and makes a deal with Onitsuka to sell Tiger running shoes in the United States.

1964 • Phil and Coach Bowerman officially launch Blue Ribbon Sports. Sales in the first year are $8,000.

1967 • Coach Bowerman designs a new shoe called the Cortez. It becomes a bestseller.

1968 • Coach Bowerman designs the Boston shoe. Sales hit $150,000. Phil marries Penny Parks and quits his job as an accounting professor to focus entirely on Blue Ribbon Sports.

1971 • Blue Ribbon Sports ends its partnership with Onitsuka. Phil decides to rename his company Nike and launches the company, along with the new Swoosh logo.

1973 • Nike signs an endorsement deal with Steve Prefontaine, a runner from the University of Oregon who goes on to set several American records. Nike sales jump to $4.8 million.

1974 • Nike launches the Nike Waffle Trainer, a running shoe with a new type of sole that Coach Bowerman invented after being inspired by the honeycomb pattern on his wife's waffle iron.

1980 • Nike goes public and passes Adidas to become the number one athletic shoe company in the United States. Sales hit $270 million.

1983 • Reebok explodes into the market as the fitness and aerobics trend surges.

1984 • Nike struggles. Many employees are laid off, and for the first time in its history, the company is not profitable. Nike signs Michael Jordan, an up-and-coming basketball star.

1985 • Nike introduces the Air Jordan I basketball shoe, along with its now famous silhouette logo.

1988 • Nike launches the Just Do It tagline.

1990 • Sales continue to grow and Nike reclaims its position as America's number one athletic shoe company.

1994 • Brazil wins the World Cup, helping Nike create a name for itself in the world of soccer.

1995 • Nike signs endorsements deals with the men's and women's U.S. soccer teams.

1996 • Nike signs a five-year $40 million deal with Tiger Woods, a golfing phenomenon. Sales top $4 billion.

1998 • The Chicago Bulls and Michael Jordan win their sixth NBA Championship since 1991.

1999 • Coach Bowerman dies at age eighty-eight, on December 24.

2001 • Sales of Nike Golf soar. Nike signs a five-year $100 million deal with Tiger Woods.

2003 • For the first time ever, Nike's international sales exceed its U.S. sales. Nike signs basketball star LeBron James for $87 million. Sales top $10 billion.

2005 • Tiger's chip shot from the rough during the Masters features a view of the Nike Swoosh on the ball as it approaches the hole, and is replayed so many times, it's valued at $1 million of free advertising. Lance Armstrong wins his seventh Tour de France title.

2008 • Nike signs Derek Jeter of the New York Yankees.

2011 • Nike sales top $20 billion.

2012 • Lance Armstrong admits to using illegal drugs. Nike ends its endorsement deal with the famous cyclist.

2015 • Phil announces he will retire and step down as Nike's chairman in 2016. Nike sales hit $30 billion.

2016 • Nike feels pressure from newer competitors like Under Armour.

2017 • Michael Jordan continues to receive $60 million from Nike each year as Air Jordan remains the best-selling basketball shoe in the world.

2018 • Phil partners with Netflix to turn the Nike story into a movie.

Nike's Top Endorsement Deals

Michael Jordan, basketball • lifetime contract of $60 million per year, plus share of Air Jordan shoe sales (for a total of $110 million per year)

LeBron James, basketball • lifetime contract of $30 million per year, plus share of LeBron shoe sales

Kevin Durant, basketball • $28.5 million per year over ten years, from 2014 to 2024

Tiger Woods, golf • $20 million per year over five years, from 2014 to 2019

Kobe Bryant, basketball • $15 million per year over five years, from 2014 to 2019

Rafael Nadal, tennis • $10 million per year over five years, from 2014 to 2019

Rory McIlroy, golf • $10 million per year over ten years, from 2013 to 2023

Source Notes

Chapter 1—Phil Knight

page

6   *"You can run fast"*: Knight, *Shoe Dog*, 18.

7   *"Besides my father"*: Ibid., 45.

11   *"Invent a new business"*: Jackie Krentzman, "Force Behind the Nike Empire," *Stanford Magazine*, January/February 1997. alumni-gsb.stanford.edu/get/page/magazine /article/?article_id=43087.

12   *"reacted with formal boredom"*: Knight, *Shoe Dog*, 10.

13   *"This is really what"*: Krentzman, "Force Behind the Nike Empire."

Chapter 2—On Your Mark, Get Set . . .

23   *$250 in profits:* Brettman, "Phil Knight's Address to the Graduating Class."

Chapter 3—Go!

35   *"No more selling someone else's brand"*: Knight, *Shoe Dog*, 208.

37   *"Hopefully, it will grow on us"*: Brettman, "Phil Knight's Address to the Graduating Class."

Chapter 4—Off to the Races

41 *fastest runner alive:* Knight, *Shoe Dog*, 163.

43 *Wayne Wells:* Nike, "Inside Access: The Nike Signature Athlete Legacy," December 2, 2014. news.nike.com/news /inside-access-the-nike-signature-athlete-legacy.

Chapter 6—Stumbling

52 *"Reebok's shoe":* Geraldine E. Willigan, "High-Performance Marketing: An Interview with Nike's Phil Knight," *Harvard Business Review,* July–August 1992.

57 *When Phil retired in 2016:* Matt Rego, "The Top 4 Nike Shareholders," June 29, 2018. investopedia.com/articles /insights/052516/top-4-nike-shareholders-nike.asp

Chapter 7—Michael Jordan: Another Perfect Fit

61 *"I don't believe in advertising":* Keller and Sichol, *Best Practice Cases in Branding,* 128.

67 *Beatles' song "Revolution":* Jack Doyle, "Nike and the Beatles, 1987–1989." PopHistoryDig.com, September 27, 2008. www.pophistorydig.com/topics/nike-and-beatles -1987-1989.

"the NBA threw them out": Darren Rovell, "How Nike Landed Michael Jordan," *ESPN,* February 15, 2013. www .espn.com/blog/playbook/dollars/post/_/id/2918/how -nike-landed-michael-jordan.

Chapter 8—Just Do It

71 *"final game of the NCAA":* Donald Katz, "Triumph of the Swoosh," *Sports Illustrated,* August 16, 1993. www.si.com/vault/1993/08/16/129105/triumph -of-the-swoosh-with-a-keen-sense-of-the-power-of -sports-and-a-genius-for-mythologizing-athletes-to -help-sell-sneakers-nike-bestrides-the-world-of-sport -like-a-marketing-colossus.

Chapter 10—Tiger Woods Drives Nike Golf

81 *"Cablinasian":* Associated Press, "Woods Stars on Oprah, Says He's 'Cablinasian.'" *Lubbock Avalanche-Journal/Associated Press.* April 23, 1997. lubbockonline .com/news/042397/woods.htm.

87 *$1 million in free advertising:* Keller and Sichol, *Best Practice Cases in Branding,* 140.

Chapter 11—Cheaters Never Win

92 *"Nike does not condone":* Nike, "Nike Statement on Lance Armstrong," October 17, 2012. news.nike.com /news/nike-statement-on-lance-armstrong.

Bibliography

Badenhausen, Kurt. "How Michael Jordan Still Earns $80 Million a Year." *Forbes*, February 14, 2013.

Brettman, Allan. "Phil Knight's Address to the Graduating Class of the Stanford Graduate School of Business, 2014." *The Oregonian*, June 17, 2014. www.oregonlive.com /playbooks-profits/index.ssf/2014/06/phil_knights _address_to_the_gr.html.

Fox, Emily Jane, and Chris Isidore. "Nike Ends Contracts with Armstrong." CNNMoney.com. October 17, 2012. money.cnn.com/2012/10/17/news/companies/nike -lance-armstrong/index.html.

Keller, Kevin Lane, and Lowey Bundy Sichol. *Best Practice Cases in Branding, Strategic Brand Management*. 3rd ed. New York: Pearson, 2007.

Knight, Phil. *Shoe Dog*. New York: Scribner, 2016.

Nike, Inc. FY2016 Annual Report.

Nike, Inc. FY2017 Annual Report.

Ripatrazone, Nick. "Story Behind Nike's Controversial 1987 'Revolution' Commercial." *Rolling Stone*, February 22, 2017.

Roth, Daniel. "Can Nike Still Do It Without Phil Knight?" *Fortune*, April 4, 2005: 59–64, 66, 68.

TotalSportek.com. "Biggest Athlete Endorsement Deals in Sports History." January 27, 2016. www.totalsportek.com /money/biggest-endorsement-deals-sports-history.

Lowey Bundy Sichol is the author of **From an Idea to . . .**, a business book series for kids. Lowey is also the founder of Case Marketing, a specialized writing firm that researches and composes case studies for business schools and corporations. Her case studies have been read by MBA students all over the world. Lowey received a BA from Hamilton College and an MBA from the Tuck School of Business at Dartmouth College. She lives in Illinois with her husband, Adam, three children, and two athletic dogs who can even climb trees. Look for her online at LoweyBundySichol.com.

FUN FACTS

Like Phil, Lowey is a runner and loves sports. She ran cross-country in high school and played softball in college. Once, in a race, her sneaker got stuck in a big pile of mud and it came off!

FUN FACTS

Lowey's favorite Nike athlete is Michael Jordan. (Makes sense—she's from Chicago.)

FUN FACTS

When Lowey was a little girl, she dreamed of becoming the first female professional baseball player. Now, she dreams one of her readers will achieve that goal.

FROM AN IDEA TO

DISNEY

How Imagination Built
a World of Magic

by **LOWEY BUNDY SICHOL**

illustrated by **C. S. JENNINGS**

FROM AN IDEA TO
GOOGLE

How Innovation at Google changed the world.

by **LOWEY BUNDY SICHOL**

illustrated by **C. S. JENNINGS**

FROM AN IDEA TO

LEGO

The Building Bricks Behind the World's Largest Toy Company

by LOWEY BUNDY SICHOL

illustrated by C. S. JENNINGS